Wild flowers

of the

Cornish coast

Trevor and Endymion Beer

Tor Mark Press • Redruth

The Tor Mark series

Birds of Cornwall
Charlestown
China clay
Classic Cornish anecdotes
Classic Cornish ghost stories
Classic folk tales from the Land's End
Classic ghost stories from the Land's End
Clotted cream
Cornish fairies
Cornish folklore
Cornish legends
Cornish mining industry
Cornish mining – underground
Cornish recipes
Cornish saints
Cornish smuggling industry
Cornwall in camera
Cornwall's engine houses
Cornwall's railways
Customs and superstitions from
  Cornish folklore
Demons, ghosts and spectres from
  Cornish folklore
Do you know Cornwall?
Down 'long weth we
Exploring Cornwall with your car
Fed fitty
Introducing Cornwall
King Arthur – man or myth?

Jan Bedella's fiddle
Lost ports of Cornwall
Old Cornwall in pictures
Pasty book
Pixy book
Shipwrecks around Land's End
Shipwrecks around the Lizard
Shipwrecks – St Ives to Bude
Short Cornish dictionary
Story of Cornwall
Story of St Ives
Story of the Cornish language
Story of Truro Cathedral
Strange tales of the Cornish coast
Tales of the Cornish smugglers
Tales of the Cornish wreckers
Twelve walks on the Lizard
What shall we do with the smuggled
  brandy?
Wild flowers of the Cornish coast

Birds of Devon
Classic Devon ghost stories
Classic West Country ghost stories
Devonshire customs and superstitions
Devonshire jokes and stories
Devonshire legends
Wild flowers of the Devon coast

First published 1999 by Tor Mark Press
United Downs Industrial Estate, St Day, Redruth, Cornwall TR16 5HY

ISBN 0-85025-377-2

© 1999 Trevor and Endymion Beer

Printed in Great Britain by R Booth (The Troutbeck Press), Mabe, Penryn, Cornwall

A fine display of Charlock, or Wild mustard

Introduction

The Westcountry cliffs and dunes that form 'the seaside' abound with wildlife species. The most noticeable of these are the many wildflowers which grace the coastal habitats with colour and scent throughout the spring and summer months.

This book identifies just some of the species which will almost certainly be found on coastal walks in Cornwall. We hope it will be an appetiser, leaving you wanting to know more about the flora of the countryside in different habitats.

We have also included some of the traditional local names, and some of the uses to which these plants have been put.

Remember to leave the plantlife for others to enjoy. Do not pick wildflowers or disturb other wild creatures. Keep to footpaths wherever possible and please remember the Country Code.

Common gorse *Ulex europaeus*

Gorse grows up to 8ft (2.5m) high and the flowers may be found at all times of the year, although April–June is when gorse flowers at its peak. It is a similar shrub to broom but gorse is covered with sharp green spines instead of leaves. The flowers are a deep rich yellow and sometimes orange.
Local names: Furze, Whin.

Ancient uses: Fuel for bakers, brick makers, lime-burners and farmers' wives. Crushed spines of gorse provided winter feed for livestock.
Habitat: Rough grassy places and heaths; prefers lighter, lime free soils.

Left: Western gorse

Western gorse
Ulex gallii

Very much a West-country gorse and smaller than the common species, growing up to 2ft (60cm). It is extremely spiny with deep golden yellow to orange flowers. The best flowering period is from July-September but it continues to flower in less profusion through-out the year, hence the saying, 'Kissing's out of season when gorse is out of bloom.'
Local names: Cornish fuzz, Tamfuzz.
Habitat: Acid soil. Rough grassland, often grows with heather.

Above: Dodder

Dodder *Cuscuta epithymum*

Thin leafless stems with tiny pinkish flowers giving an overall reddish appearance, twining anti-clockwise, usually over gorse and heather. A parasite attached by suckers to the stems of host species. Locally common, July-October.
Local names: Lady's laces, Strangle weed, Adder's cotton.
Ancient uses: Against scabies, and as a purgative.
Habitat: Coastal cliffs and heaths wherever its host plants grow. Only found actually growing over the host plants in a 'tangle'.

Traveller's joy *Clematis vitalba*

A rampant deciduous plant which climbs by twisting its leaf stalks around the stems of the other plants. Like honeysuckle, the stems become thick and woody with age. The flowers are a whitish green or cream colour and are fragrantly sweet. Flowering period July–September.

Local names: Old man's beard, Gipsy's bacca.

Ancient uses: Lengths of the dry stems were smoked years ago. Also rubbed on travellers' bruises to ease aches and pains.

Habitat: Scrub, woodland, old walls, hedgerows. Mostly on calcareous soil.

Dog rose *Rosa canina*

There are several different species of dog rose which are not easy to distinguish. The flowers are pink or white and sweetly scented. The dog rose is a common shrub and a vigorous climber with

Above: Great willowherb

hooked prickles on the stems. The flowering time is from June-July.
Ancient uses: Roots were used to cure dog bites. Hips were used to make rosehip jelly and rosehip syrup, rich in vitamin C.
Habitat: Hedgerows, scrubland and thickets.

Great willowherb *Epilobium hirsutum*

Great willowherb is very hairy, stout, and grows from 32–72in (80–180cm). The leaves are coarsely toothed and mostly opposite. The flowers are a bright purplish pink and blossom from July-August.
Local names: Codlins-and-cream (from the smell of the leaves when a little bruised: codlings are a kind of apple).
Habitat: Cultivated wasteland, woodlands, ditches, rocky places and common by stream sides and damp places.

Above: Herb Robert

Herb Robert
Geranium robertianum

An annual with hairy stems and leaves which are green tinged and red, sometimes completely red. The leaves are fern shaped and the flowers pink. It's a strong smelling herb and grows from 4–20in (10–50cm). Flowering time May-September.
Local names: Bachelor's buttons, Gipsy flower, Gipsies.
Ancient uses: To treat blood disorders. Leaves were used to staunch the flow of blood.
Habitat: Hedgebanks, woodlands, old walls, rocky and coastal habitats.

Houndstongue *Cynoglossum officinale*
Houndstongue is a biennial and grows up to 16–28in (40–70cm) high. It is covered with long silky hairs and is soft to touch. The flowers are blood red-purple and blossom from June to August. The name 'Houndstongue' relates to the shape of the leaves.
Ancient uses: Used against dog bites, burns, baldness, internal sores and ulcers, skin diseases and piles.
Habitat: Waste ground or by roadsides and hedges, edges of woods, sand dunes and downs by the sea.

Above left: Wall pennywort   *Above right: Houndstongue*

Wall pennywort *Umbilicus rupestris*
Wall pennywort grows between 6-16in (15-40cm) in height.
The larger specimens are usually found growing in damp shady
places. It is a perennial and flowers from June to August. The
flowers are small, bell-shaped, cream or pale greenish white.
The leaves are round and fleshy.
Local names: Navel wort, Cups-and-saucers, Penny loaves.
Ancient uses: Against cuts, chilblains, inflamation and 'the
stone'.
Habitat: It is fairly common on walls, rocks and even among
the moss on oak trees.

Ling or Heather
Calluna vulgaris

Small shrub usually under 2ft (60cm) high; branched stems rooting at the base. The tiny opposite leaves may be smooth or hairy. Colour, from pink to purple, occasionally white – the 'lucky white heather'. The flowers are visited by bees and other insects, heather honey being a popular food in Cornwall. The hive bees are often taken to the heather when it is in full flower, from July to September. *Local names:* Bazzom, Griglans.

Above: Ling   Below: Bell heather

Kidney vetch
Anthyllis vulneraria

Low growing plant with typical vetch leaves in opposites along the stem with a single leaf at the end. When growing near the sea the flowers may vary from pale yellow to orange and fiery red. Flowers May to August.
Local name: Lamb's foot.
Ancient uses: Known throughout Europe as a wound herb, or 'vulnerary'.
Habitat: Often common in dry grassy places near the sea and may carpet whole areas in golden patches.

Above: Kidney vetch – not to be confused with Bird's foot trefoil, see page 15

Bell heather *Erica cinerea*

Low evergreen shrub up to 2ft (60cm); similar to Ling in habit. Smooth leaves in whorls of three with short shoots in the leaf axils. The bell-shaped corolla tube has 8 stamens hidden inside. The flowers are pollinated by bees. Usually a strongly rich purple and often growing with Ling.
Habitat: Heaths and moorland, helping turn the landscape purple along with Ling.

Wood sage *Teucrium scorodonia*

Upright, with spikes of greenish-yellow flowers which, unlike the rest of the family, have no upper lip, so the stamens are quite prominent. Grows to about 1ft (30cm) high with toothed leaves growing opposite in pairs up the stem. July to September.

Ancient uses: As a tea against rheumatism, and as a diuretic, a wound herb and a herb against broken veins, ulcers and scurvy. Used in brewing as a bitter before ales and beers were hopped.

Habitat: Common in grasslands, heaths, dunes and coastal areas, preferring dry, shady places with acid soils.

Left: Wood sage   Below: Cow-wheat

Alexanders

Smyrnium olusatrum

Rare inland but not uncommon around the coastal areas. A tall biennial 2ft–4ft (60–120cm) high with solid, furrowed stems which have a celery taste when young. Flowers are more yellow than most umbellifers and the fruits are almost black and sharply ribbed. April-June.

Local names: Allsanders, Skit, Skeet.

Ancient uses: An ancient pot herb, originally naturalised from the Mediterranean.

Habitat: Cliffs and waste places near the sea.

Above: Alexanders

Cow-wheat *Melampyrum pratense*

Common Cow-wheat has the distinguishing characteristic that all its flowers face the same way. The colour range is from deep yellow to almost white, the plant being from 6–12in (15–30cm) tall. All the cow-wheats are semi-parasites, i.e they grow attached to other plant roots and obtain part of their nourishment from them. Flowers May-September.

Ancient uses: Cow-wheat flour was believed to be an aphrodisiac; some believed it caused women to give birth to boys.

Habitat: Common in woods and on moors and found around the coast in the vicinity of trees.

Above: Red field poppy
Below: Bird's foot trefoil

Red field poppy
Papaver rhoeas

Growing up to 2ft (60cm) with spreading hairs on the leaves and flowers stalks. The two hairy sepals covering the bud drop off as the flower opens. Bright scarlet flowers. The 'Poppy Day' poppy, once common in corn fields but mostly destroyed by weed killers. Flowers June to August.

Local names: Corn poppy, Devil's tongue, Wart flower.

Ancient uses: Used to cure headaches; placed in roof timbers to ward off lightning. Once thought of as the inseparable companion to corn.

Habitat: Around coastal waste places and field edges.

Tormentil
Potentilla erecta

Leaves divided into 3 toothed leaflets with 2 basal leaf-like stipules, giving a 5 fingered effect. Flowers almost always have 4 sepals and petals, the plant having a low growing habit though the stems never form roots. Bright yellow flowers, May–September.
Ancient uses: Roots boiled in milk to treat diarrhoea in children and calves. Also for tanning leather and for a red dye.
Habitat: Moors, heaths and grassy areas on acid soils. Common around the coast.

Above: Tormentil

Bird's foot trefoil *Lotus corniculatus*

A brightly golden flower often tinged flame-like; with leaves with five oval leaflets, the lowest leaflet pair close to the stem, distant from the other three. Flowers in 'heads' of 3–8, June-August.
Local names: Boots and shoes, Tom Thumb (Tom Thumb being associated with goblins). There are in all over 100 local names for this plant in Britain!
Habitat: Dry grassland areas, the plant carpeting the coastal walks in parts of Cornwall.

Viper's bugloss
Echium vulgare

Tall vivid blue biennial 1–3ft (30–90cm) high, covered with white bristly hairs. Rosettes of large, stalked leaves may wither before flowering. Flowers have pink buds. Visited by insects for nectar. June–September.
Name: It is named 'Viper's' because the nutlets resemble a viper's head; also possibly because the stalks are speckled like snakeskin.
Ancient uses: Against snake bite, sadness and melancholy.
Habitat: Common in coastal dunes.

Above: Viper's bugloss

Thrift *Armeria maritima*

Tufted perennial with rosettes of grass-like leaves, hairy flowering stems without leaves and solitary pink flower-heads. All parts of individual flowers in fives. March-October.
Local names: Sea pink, Tab mawn, Sea daisy.
Habitat: Common on cliffs and in muddy or sandy places along the coast. Often found carpeting large areas of cliffs.

Sea campion *Silene maritima*

Perennial, woody at the base with outward spreading stems, growing along the ground. Leaves smaller and stiffer than

Above: Thrift

Bladder campion, with fewer long-stalked flowers on each stem. Not to be confused with white forms of the Red campion which occasionally occur in Cornwall. Flowers May-September.
Habitat: Common around the coastal cliffs and shingly beach areas. Patches of the plant will be found along the South-west Coast Path areas.

Right: Sea campion

Ragwort
Senecio jacobaea

Perennial growing to 4ft (120cm) tall with a rosette of large divided leaves at the base which often dies before the plant flowers. Officially a noxious weed but not usually eaten by animals, it grows with bright yellow flowers in pastures and waste land all around the coast. It is the main foodplant of the cinnabar moth, a black and vermilion day flying species with black and gold striped larva.

Above: Ragwort
Below: English stonecrop

Ragwort flowers from June to October.
Habitat: Grassy areas around the coast including dune slacks.

White clover, also known as **Dutch clover** *Trifolium repens*
Small, hairless perennial with creeping and rooting stems. Finely toothed leaflets show a pale band across. Very common.
Local names: Bobby-roses, Mull, Quillet, Three-leaved grass.
Habitat: Grassy places.

Above: White clover

English stonecrop *Sedum anglicum*
Small perennial with erect flowering stems and creeping non-flowering stems just a few inches high and with fleshy, hairless leaves. Flowers white, often pink tinged and almost unstalked. These have 5 sepals, petals and carpels and 10 stamens. June-August.
Habitat: Rocky places and bare ground, non-calcareous (non-limestone) sandy soils, dunes and shingle.

Scentless mayweed
Matricaria inodora

Perennial with hairless leaves and smooth spreading stem up to 2ft (60cm) long. White, large daisy flower-heads the bracts around which are brown edged. July-September.
Habitats: Often common in grassy places.

Knapweed
Centaurea nigra

Perennial with tough, branching stems 1–2ft (30–60cm) high, the larger and lower leaves slightly toothed. Can be distinguished from thistles by the leaves which are not prickly. Bright purple. Flowers June-September.
Local name: Hardheads.
Ancient uses: For wounds and ruptures, bruises, sores and sore throats. Also used by country girls to foretell future lovers.
Habitat: Waysides and coastal fields.

Top: Scentless mayweed
Middle: Knapweed
Bottom: Common scurvy grass

Common scurvy grass
Cochlearia officinalis

Low growing plant with four-petalled white flowers and smooth, fleshy leaves which contain vitamin C. Flowers May-August.
Ancient uses: Against scurvy, both as a medicine and in sandwiches.
Habitat: Common along roadsides and often carpeting saltmarshes and coastal estuarine sites.

Tree mallow
Lavatera arborea

Stout biennial with stems woody at the base. May grow to 10ft (300cm). Soft hairy leaves are slightly lobed. Petals are purple with darker purple veins. The yellowish fruits have wrinkled surfaces. Flowers July-September.
Ancient uses: Against sprains, 'steeped in water and laid on the injury'.
Habitat: Sea cliffs.

Tree mallow

Left: Sea holly   *Right: Great mullein*

Sea holly *Eryngium maritimum*

Sea holly is a pale bluish green colour and is rather thistle-like.
The leaves have whitish veins and edges and there is a leathery
texture in both stalk and leaves. This is caused by a thick outer
skin, or cuticle, which prevents the plant from losing any great
amount of water, and protects against salt spray. It grows at a
height of 12–24in (30–60cm). The flower heads are made up of
clustered tiny blue flowers. Flowering period July–August.
Ancient uses: The roots were candied and sold as a delicacy
called 'eringoes'. Eringoes were used as an aphrodisiac as well
as to help restore the health of elderly folk.
Habitat: Sand shingle and occasionally found among rocks but
widespread and local by the sea.

Evening primrose
Oenothera biennis

Erect, usually
unbranched, tall,
2–3 $^1/_2$ ft (60–100cm).
Leaves oval, lance-
shaped, often toothed.
Flowers saucer-shaped,
bright yellow and
large, usually falling
after a day's blooming
to be replaced by
others.
Ancient uses: Against
whooping cough,
asthma, female
complaints, gastro-
intestinal disorders.
Habitat: Sandy places
around the coast.

Above: Evening primrose flower

Great mullein *Verbascum thapsus*

Great mullein is the largest of the mullein family growing from
3 $^1/_4$ – 6 $^1/_2$ ft (1–2m). It is a biennial and flowers from June-
August. It has yellow flowers which are clustered to form a
narrow spike. The whole plant is covered with whitish or
greyish soft hairs.
Habitat: Found on dry soils in sunny places particularly in
rough dry grassland and waste sites, banks, stony places, roadsides and hedgerows.

Above: Restharrow

Restharrow *Ononis repens*

Hairy perennial with bright pink flowers and low growing habit, and woody, often creeping root system, sometimes spiny. A weed of cultivation, it was known for 'arresting-the-harrow', hence its English name. Stipules covered with spiny hairs and attached to leaf stalks. June–September.

Local name: Cammock.

Ancient uses: The roots were chewed by children as 'Wild liquorice'.

Habitat: Grasslands and sand dune systems.

Rock spurrey *Spergularia rupicola*

Glandular, hairy stems, silvery stipules and petals about the same length as the sepals. Pink. Also known as Cliff sand spurrey.

Habitat: Found around rocky coasts and in dune systems.

Carline thistle *Carlina vulgaris*

Biennial with purplish flowering stem growing to 12in (30cm) and carrying 1–5 flower heads. The stiff shiny inner bracts spread about the flower-head like ray florets to close up at night or in bad weather. July–September.

Habitat: Found in sand dune systems.

Above: Rock spurrey   *Below: Carline thistle*

Above: Wild pansy   *Below: Sea bindweed*

Wild pansy *Viola tricolor*

Varies from yellow to purple in colour. At the bottom of each leaf stalk are leafy, deeply cut stipules. The variously coloured flowers are typically pansy-like, or better likened to large violets. May-September.

Local names: Heart'sease.

Habitat: May be common in waste areas, wet slacks and cornfield edges around the coast.

Sea bindweed *Calystegia soldanella*

Large trumpet-like flowers of the typical convolvulus. Creeping, not climbing, stems, small rounded leaves and pink flowers. June–August.

Habitat: Common in sand dune areas.

Portland spurge
Euphorbia portlandica

Less tall and robust than the similar Sea spurge, and greyer in colour. Leaves are small, lance shaped ('lanceolate'), pointed and leathery. Look for reddish stems. June-October.

Habitat: Sand dunes and sea shores.

Right: Portland spurge

Sea spurge
Euphorbia paralias

The pale green leaves of this perennial are thick, fleshy and crowded together on the stems. Flower clusters have 3-6 main branches and the rounded bracts are also thick and fleshy. June–October.
Habitat: Sand dunes and sea shores.

Wild thyme *Thymus drucei*

Low growing, sweet smelling perennial with long creeping stems. Squarish flower stems have dense hairs on 2 opposite faces and the leaves are hairy edged. Rich purple flowers, June–September.
Ancient uses: The tea to prevent bad dreams. Against gripes, and a uterine herb. To cure headaches and giddiness. The scent gives strength and courage.
Habitat: Heaths and dry grassy places, cliffs and dunes.

Yellow stonecrop *Sedum acre*

Bright yellow flowers, the plant forming mats of short stems 2–4in (5–10cm) tall, strikingly yellow and the commonest and smallest of the yellow stonecrops. Flowers June–July.
Local name: Wall pepper. *Acre* in the Latin name means bitter, from the acrid or biting taste.
Ancient uses: Against scurvy, dropsy and some fevers.
Habitat: Sandy places around the coast, and rocks near the sea.

Above: Wild thyme   *Below: Yellow stonecrop*

Sea stock (facing page)
Matthiola sinuata

A pale lilac flowered herbaceous plant with thick fleshy stems of greyish-green. Lower leaves have a deep, wavy outline and are notched or toothed. Widely or loosely spreading and local. Flowers May-August. *Habitat:* Shores and sea cliffs.

Sea rocket
Cakile maritima

Grows to 2ft (60cm) tall, leaves fleshy and blue-green. Flowers pink, violet or whitish and scented. Flowers June-September. *Habitat:* Seashores.

Yellow wort
Blackstonia perfoliata

Stem leaves grow in pairs joined together around the stems. Flowers bright yellow. June-October. *Ancient uses:* Against cholera. *Habitat:* Chalk and lime-stone turf.

Above: Sea rocket Below: Yellow wort

Index